DIAGNOSING ORGANIZATIONAL CULTURE

Organizational culture is the pattern of beliefs, values, rituals, myths, and sentiments shared by the members of an organization. It influences the behavior of all individuals and groups within the organization. Culture impacts most aspects of organizational life, such as how decisions are made, who makes them, how rewards are distributed, who is promoted, how people are treated, how the organization responds to its environment, and so on. This instrument is designed to help you and other members of your organization to identify aspects of your organization's culture.

Instructions for Completing the Instrument

This instrument contains 15 "beginnings" of sentences that describe some aspect of organizational functioning and design. Following each of the beginnings are four possible "endings." Combined with the beginning, each ending will form a complete sentence describing one of four different patterns of organizational behavior, beliefs, values, etc.

In the underlined spaces below the heading EXISTING CULTURE, rank order the phrases following each sentence beginning. Do this by placing a "4" in front of the ending phrase that you think comes closest to describing the way things *are* in your organization, a "3" in front of the one that comes the next closest, and so on through "2" and "1"—the one that least describes the way things are in your organization.

Complete all fifteen items in the same way, by ranking the four alternatives. Then go back to the spaces below the PREFERRED CULTURE heading and rank the phrases again, but this time rank them according to the way you would *like* things to be in your organization. Give a "4" to your most preferred option, a "3" to your next most preferred, and so on through "2" and "1"—the option you prefer least.

DIAGNOSING ORGANIZATIONAL CULTURE

Please check your answers to be sure that you have assigned only one "4," one "3," one "2," and one "1" for each phrase in the "existing" column and for each phrase in the "preferred" column.

Ranking key:

> 4 = The dominant view, or your most preferred alternative.
>
> 3 = The next most dominant view or preferred alternative.
>
> 2 = The next most dominant view or preferred alternative.
>
> 1 = The least dominant view or least preferred alternative.

EXISTING PREFERRED
CULTURE CULTURE

1. **Members of the organization are expected to give first priority to**

   _____ _____ a. meeting the needs and demands of their supervisors and other high-level people in the organization.

   _____ _____ b. carrying out the duties of their own jobs; staying within the policies and procedures related to their jobs.

   _____ _____ c. meeting the challenges of the task, finding a better way to do things.

   _____ _____ d. cooperating with the people with whom they work, to solve work and personal problems.

2. **People who do well in the organization tend to be those who**

   _____ _____ a. know how to please their supervisors and are able and willing to use power and politics to get ahead.

   _____ _____ b. play by the rules, work within the system, and strive to do things correctly.

   _____ _____ c. are technically competent and effective, with a strong commitment to getting the job done.

   _____ _____ d. build close working relationships with others by being cooperative, responsive, and caring.

3.   The organization treats individuals

_____ _____ a. as "hands" whose time and energy are at the disposal of persons at higher levels in the hierarchy.

_____ _____ b. as "employees" whose time and energy are purchased through a contract, with rights and obligations for both sides.

_____ _____ c. as "associates" or peers who are mutually committed to the achievement of a common purpose.

_____ _____ d. as "family" or "friends" who like being together and who care about and support one another.

4.   People are managed, directed, or influenced by

_____ _____ a. people in positions of authority, who exercise their power through the use of rewards and punishments.

_____ _____ b. the systems, rules, and procedures that prescribe what people should do and the right ways of doing it.

_____ _____ c. their own commitment to achieving the goals of the organization.

_____ _____ d. their own desire to be accepted by others and to be good members of their work group.

5.   Decision-making processes are characterized by

_____ _____ a. directives, orders, and instructions that come down from higher levels.

_____ _____ b. the adherence to formal channels and reliance on policies and procedures for making decisions.

_____ _____ c. decisions being made close to the point of action, by the people on the spot.

_____ _____ d. the use of consensus decision-making methods to gain acceptance and support for decisions.

6.   Assignments of tasks or jobs to individuals are based on

_____ _____ a. the personal judgments, values, and wishes of those in positions of power.

_____ _____ b. the needs and plans of the organization and the rules of the system (seniority, qualifications, etc.).

Diagnosing Organizational Culture

_____   _____   c. matching the requirements of the job with the interests and abilities of the individuals.

_____   _____   d. the personal preferences of the individuals and their needs for growth and development.

7. **Employees are expected to be**

_____   _____   a. hard-working, compliant, obedient, and loyal to the interests of those to whom they report.

_____   _____   b. responsible and reliable, carrying out the duties and responsibilities of their jobs and avoiding actions that could surprise or embarrass their supervisors.

_____   _____   c. self-motivated and competent, willing to take the initiative to get things done; willing to challenge those to whom they report if that is necessary to obtain good results.

_____   _____   d. good team workers, supportive and cooperative, who get along well with others.

8. **Managers and supervisors are expected to be**

_____   _____   a. strong and decisive; firm but fair.

_____   _____   b. impersonal and proper, avoiding the exercise of authority for their own advantage.

_____   _____   c. democratic and willing to accept subordinates' ideas about the task.

_____   _____   d. supportive, responsive, and concerned about the personal concerns and needs of those whose work they supervise.

9. **It is considered legitimate for one person to tell another what to do when**

_____   _____   a. he or she has more power, authority, or "clout" in the organization.

_____   _____   b. it is part of the responsibilities included in his or her job description.

_____   _____   c. he or she has greater knowledge and expertise and uses it to guide the other person or to teach him or her to do the work.

_____   _____   d. the other person asks for his or her help, guidance, or advice.

4

10. **Work motivation is primarily the result of**

_____ _____ a. hope for rewards, fear of punishment, or personal loyalty to the supervisor.

_____ _____ b. acceptance of the norm of providing a "fair day's work for a fair day's pay."

_____ _____ c. strong desires to achieve, to create, and to innovate and peer pressure to contribute to the success of the organization.

_____ _____ d. people wanting to help others and to develop and maintain satisfying working relationships.

11. **Relationships between work groups or departments are generally**

_____ _____ a. competitive, with both looking out for their own interests and helping each other only when they can see some advantage for themselves by doing so.

_____ _____ b. characterized by indifference toward each other, helping each other only when it is convenient or when they are directed by higher levels to do so.

_____ _____ c. cooperative when they need to achieve common goals. People are normally willing to cut red tape and cross organizational boundaries in order to get the job done.

_____ _____ d. friendly, with a high level of responsiveness to requests for help from other groups.

12. **Intergroup and interpersonal conflicts are usually**

_____ _____ a. dealt with by the personal intervention of people at higher levels of authority.

_____ _____ b. avoided by reference to rules, procedures, and formal definitions of authority and responsibility.

_____ _____ c. resolved through discussions aimed at getting the best outcomes possible for the work issues involved.

_____ _____ d. dealt with in a manner that maintains good working relationships and minimizes the chances of people being hurt.

13. **The larger environment outside the organization is responded to as though it were**

_____ _____ a. a jungle, where the organization is in competition for survival with others.

_____ _____ b. an orderly system in which relationships are determined by structures and procedures and where everyone is expected to abide by the rules.

_____ _____ c. a competition for excellence in which productivity, quality, and innovation bring success.

_____ _____ d. a community of interdependent parts in which the common interests are the most important.

14. **If rules, systems, or procedures get in the way, people**

_____ _____ a. break them if they have enough clout to get by with it or if they think they can get away with it without being caught.

_____ _____ b. generally abide by them or go through proper channels to get permission to deviate from them or have them changed.

_____ _____ c. tend to ignore or by-pass them to accomplish their tasks or perform their jobs better.

_____ _____ d. support one another in ignoring or bending them if they are felt to be unfair or to create hardships for others.

15. **New people in the organization need to learn**

_____ _____ a. who really runs things; who can help or hurt them; whom to avoid offending; the norms (unwritten rules) that have to be observed if they are to stay out of trouble.

_____ _____ b. the formal rules and procedures and to abide by them; to stay within the formal boundaries of their jobs.

_____ _____ c. what resources are available to help them do their jobs; to take the initiative to apply their skills and knowledge to their jobs.

_____ _____ d. how to cooperate; how to be good team members; how to develop good working relationships with others.

6

Instructions for Scoring the Instrument

When you have finished ranking the sentences, tear out the Scoring Sheet on page 9 of this booklet and transfer the rankings that you gave each item onto it. Then follow the instructions provided at the top of the Scoring Sheet to total your scores. The totals for each column can be used to construct a bar chart that will show the profiles of your "existing" and "desired" organizational cultures.

If others from your organization also have filled out the instrument, you may find it of interest to compare your scores, to determine the range and average of your scores, and to use the information to construct a second bar chart showing the group averages. Forms for constructing both individual and group profiles are provided on pages 11 and 12 of this booklet.

When you have entered and totaled your scores, please complete the "Information for Organizational Culture Database" on the reverse side of the Scoring Sheet.

Interpreting Your Scores

After you have completed the instrument and scored your answers, turn to page 13, "Understanding Your Organization's Culture," for an explanation of the four-culture model on which this instrument is based. This material will help you to understand the significance of your scores. It also will provide useful topics for discussions of organizational culture with your associates.

SCORING SHEET

Instructions: Enter your rankings of your organization's culture in the spaces below. Place your scores describing the Existing Culture on the left; enter your scores describing your Preferred Culture on the right. After you transfer your answers, total each column and enter the sums in the appropriate spaces. Be sure that there is only one "4," one "3," one "2," and one "1" for each statement in the Existing column, and the same for the Preferred column.

	EXISTING CULTURE				PREFERRED CULTURE		
1a ___	1b ___	1c ___	1d ___	1a ___	1b ___	1c ___	1d ___
2a ___	2b ___	2c ___	2d ___	2a ___	2b ___	2c ___	2d ___
3a ___	3b ___	3c ___	3d ___	3a ___	3b ___	3c ___	3d ___
4a ___	4b ___	4c ___	4d ___	4a ___	4b ___	4c ___	4d ___
5a ___	5b ___	5c ___	5d ___	5a ___	5b ___	5c ___	5d ___
6a ___	6b ___	6c ___	6d ___	6a ___	6b ___	6c ___	6d ___
7a ___	7b ___	7c ___	7d ___	7a ___	7b ___	7c ___	7d ___
8a ___	8b ___	8c ___	8d ___	8a ___	8b ___	8c ___	8d ___
9a ___	9b ___	9c ___	9d ___	9a ___	9b ___	9c ___	9d ___
10a ___	10b ___	10c ___	10d ___	10a ___	10b ___	10c ___	10d ___
11a ___	11b ___	11c ___	11d ___	11a ___	11b ___	11c ___	11d ___
12a ___	12b ___	12c ___	12d ___	12a ___	12b ___	12c ___	12d ___
13a ___	13b ___	13c ___	13d ___	13a ___	13b ___	13c ___	13d ___
14a ___	14b ___	14c ___	14d ___	14a ___	14b ___	14c ___	14d ___
15a ___	15b ___	15c ___	15d ___	15a ___	15b ___	15c ___	15d ___

Totals ___ ___ ___ ___   ___ ___ ___ ___

     (P)   (R)   (A)   (S)   (P)   (R)   (A)   (S)

Now compute your Culture Index Scores for both the Existing and Preferred scales by adding the (A) and (S) scores and subtracting the (P) and (R) scores:

Existing Culture Index = (A) _____ + (S) _____ - (P) _____ - (R) _____ = _____

Preferred Culture Index = (A) _____ + (S) _____ - (P) _____ - (R) _____ = _____

Transfer these totals onto the Organizational Culture Profiles form on page 11. Make sure you have filled out the reverse side of this Scoring Sheet and save it for later use.

Information for Organizational Culture Database

Harrison Associates asks all professional users of this instrument to provide copies of their answer sheets, from which we are building a database of comparative organizational-culture profiles. We will classify your scores according to the type of organization you are in and the kind of work you do. This information will aid research on how organizational cultures differ in different national cultures.

The information you give will be used for scientific purposes only and is not designed to identify persons with their instrument responses. Should you have concerns about the confidentiality of your responses, please discuss them with the professional who is helping you use this instrument. If you are then still uncomfortable about giving us this information, leave out as much of it as you need in order to feel at ease.

1. In what country is your organization located?

    _____

2. What services, functions, or kinds of products does your organization provide?

    _____

3. What function does your unit perform within the organization? (E.g., operations, human resource services, sales, marketing.)

    _____

4. What kind of work do you do?

    _____

5. Which of the following would most accurately describe your current organizational level?

    a. ___ Top management

    b. ___ Middle management

    c. ___ First-line supervision

    d. ___ Direct work

    e. ___ Staff

    f. ___ Other: _____

Please send copies of completed Scoring Sheets and Database Information to:

Roger Harrison, Ph. D.
Harrison Associates
3646 East Redtail Lane
Clinton, WA 98236
Telephone (360) 579-1805; FAX (360) 579-1805

ORGANIZATIONAL CULTURE PROFILES

Sums of Personal Rankings

Instructions: Draw a line on the chart below that shows the sums of your individual scores for both **Existing** and **Preferred** cultures, then shade in the spaces below the lines that you drew. The shaded lines in each column show the average of the scores of a sample of 190 mid-level managers. Also mark your culture index for both **Existing** and **Preferred** cultures.

INDIVIDUAL CHART

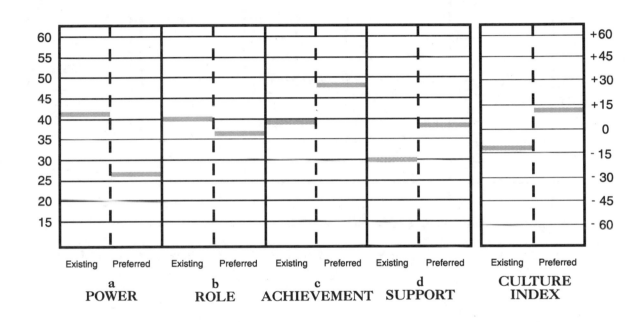

Average of the Sums of Group Rankings

Instructions: Add the scores of everyone in your group for each category (P, R, A, and S) and divide by the number of members in your group to obtain the average for the group. Draw a line on the chart below that shows these average sums for both **Existing** and **Preferred** cultures, then shade in the spaces below the lines that you drew. The average culture index is computed in the same way that the individual culture index was determined, except the group average scores are used instead of individual scores. The shaded lines in each column show the average of the scores of a sample of 190 mid-level managers.

GROUP CHART

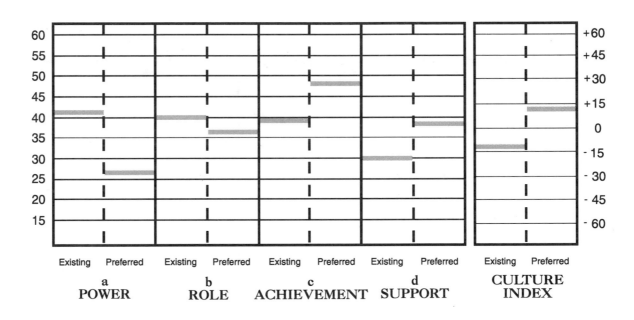

Diagnosing Organizational Culture

UNDERSTANDING YOUR ORGANIZATION'S CULTURE

What Is Organizational Culture?

An organization's culture is made up of those aspects of the organization that give it a particular climate or feel. *Culture* is to an organization what *personality* is to an individual. It is that distinctive constellation of beliefs, values, work styles, and relationships that distinguish one organization from another.

What Does the Instrument Measure?

There are many different aspects of organizational culture about which we might inquire. This instrument looks at how people treat one another, what values they live by, how people are motivated to produce, and how people use power in the organization. These things are at the core of what most people mean when they speak of their organization's culture.

Now that you have filled out our instrument, you already may have a good idea of what it measures. All the (a) alternatives refer to an organizational culture called *Power*-oriented. The (b) alternatives assess the *Role* culture; the (c) alternatives describe a culture based on *Achievement;* and the (d) alternatives describe a *Support* orientation.

Every organization has some combination of these four basic organizational cultures. Each evokes different behaviors and is based on different human values. Each involves a unique way of making decisions, a characteristic way of motivating people to work, a typical management style, and a set of underlying values and beliefs about work and about human nature. The four cultures are only partially compatible with one another, and the benefits of one can only be achieved at the expense of some of the benefits of the others. The following pages describe each of these cultures and explain the benefits and drawbacks of each.

The Power Orientation

The Power-oriented organization is based on inequality of access to resources. A *resource* can be anything one person controls that another person wants. In business, some "currencies" of power are money, privileges, job security, working conditions, and the ability to control others' access to these. The people in power use resources to satisfy or frustrate the needs of others and, thus, to control others' behavior. Leadership resides in the person of the leader(s) and rests on the leader's ability and willingness to administer rewards and punishments. People in power-oriented organizations are motivated by rewards and punishments and by the wish to be associated with a strong leader.

In the Power organization at its best, leadership is based on strength, justice, and paternalistic benevolence on the part of the leader. The leaders are firm, fair, and generous with loyal subordinates. They have a sense of obligation to their followers and they exercise power according to their understanding of what is good for the organization and all its people. This orientation toward the use of responsible power seems to be typical of some of the best Asian and Latin American organizations. It rests on the acceptance of hierarchy and inequality as legitimate by all members of the organization. In more industrialized democracies, such as the United States, there is much less acceptance of hierarchy as being legitimate than there is in more traditional societies, and there is not a strong cultural value to reinforce benevolent, power-oriented leadership.

At its worst, the Power-oriented organization tends toward a rule by fear, with abuse of power for personal advantage on the part of the leaders, their friends, and their proteges. When the organization becomes large, or when the leaders struggle for dominance, it may degenerate into a hotbed of political intrigue.

The Power orientation is well-suited to entrepreneurial and start-up situations in which leaders have the vision, intelligence, and will to manage the business and assume personal direction of the activities of its people. The other people in the organization extend the leaders' reach, leverage, and impact. There is a personal relationship between leaders and followers. The latter depend on their leaders for direction and security, and the leaders depend on followers for loyal service.

As the size and complexity of the business increases, the demands on the leadership of a Power-oriented organization multiply exponentially. Large Power-oriented organizations are inefficient and full of fear and confusion, unless the power orientation is supplemented by good structures and systems for getting work done. As the distance between leaders and followers increases, effective control becomes more difficult. When Power-oriented organizations expand, they often run short of leadership talent, because followers have been conditioned to be dependent.

The Role Orientation

The Role culture substitutes a system of structures and procedures for the naked power of the leaders. Structures and systems give protection to subordinates and stability to the organization. The struggle for power is moderated by the rule of law. The duties and the rewards of members' roles are carefully defined, usually in writing, and are the subject of an explicit or implicit contract between the organization and the individual. People perform specific functions in order to receive defined rewards. Both the individual and the organization are expected to adhere to their parts of the bargain.

The values of the Role orientation are order, dependability, rationality, and consistency. A well-designed system of roles (a bureaucracy) in which performance is organized by structures and procedures—rather than personally controlled by the leader—permits work to be reliably directed at a distance, so that large, complex organizations can be created and managed. Authority and responsibility are delegated downward. Each level in the organization has a defined area of authority, and work can continue to be done without direct supervision from the top.

At its best, the Role-oriented organization provides stability, justice, and efficient performance. Under the rules, people receive protection from the arbitrary exercise of authority that is typical of the Power orientation. People are able to spend less time looking out for themselves and can devote more energy to their work.

Traditional Role-oriented organizations are best adapted to the stable combinations of technology, supplies, and markets that characterized the century between 1850 and 1950. In rapidly changing situations, they have difficulty keeping up with circumstances. Nevertheless, most large organizations today have strong elements of the Role culture. Our society probably would fall apart without it.

The weakness of Role organizations is in the very impersonality that is their strength. They operate on the assumption that people are not to be trusted, so they do not give individual autonomy or discretion to members at lower levels. The system is designed to control people and to prevent them from committing selfish or stupid acts. It also keeps people from being innovative and from doing the right thing when the right thing is outside the rules. In the interests of rationality and order, it is difficult to change or bend the rules, and it usually takes a long time to make needed changes.

New approaches to management such as *employee involvement* and *total quality management* (TQM) attempt to blend the Role orientation's emphasis on well-designed and closely managed systems with the empowerment of employees that is typical of the Achievement orientation. These approaches endeavor to make the system serve the workers and, thus, to combine the economic effectiveness of the Role orientation with the high energy of the Achievement culture.

The Achievement Orientation

Both the Power-oriented and the Role-oriented organizational cultures depend on the use of external rewards and punishments to motivate people. Organization members are expected to contribute their personal energy in return for rewards. This means that the organization has available to it only that fraction of each person's personal energy that he or she is willing to commit in return for the extrinsic rewards the organization offers.

However, many people like their work, want to make a worthwhile contribution to society, and enjoy interacting with colleagues or customers. These intrinsic rewards are qualitative rather than quantitative and arise from the nature of the work and/or the context in which it takes place. Traditional Power- and Role-oriented organizations are not designed to provide such intrinsic satisfactions, and their presence is either the result of chance or through the occupational choices people make on their own.

In some work situations, these intrinsic satisfactions arise naturally. Others are deliberately built into the job and the work climate. People who have worked in such diverse situations as new business and new plant start-ups, nuclear test shots, intensive care units, and political and community organizing campaigns report that these work cultures can provide deep personal satisfactions and evoke personal commitment of a high order. These high-energy work situations have been described by participants in the following ways:

- The work situation engages the total person.

- The values that people experience in the work transcend personal advantage. The situation evokes altruism, which is satisfying to everyone involved. People feel they are working for something bigger than themselves.

- People give their all, working long hours without complaint. They may willingly sacrifice their family and social lives to the demands of the work.

- People supervise themselves, seeking out what needs to be done without direction from above.

- There is high morale, teamwork, and a sense of camaraderie. The group frequently feels itself to be elite or special.

- There is a sense of urgency; people live on the edge, putting out high energy for long periods of time. They may become addicted to stress.

- There is a clearly understood mission that is articulated at the highest level of the organization.

- The mission is emphasized and reinforced by everything upper managers do: the financial decisions they make; the questions they ask and the topics they pursue in meetings; the sorts of people they hire, fire, and promote; and the aspects of the operation they look at during field visits.

- The mission is stated in unambiguous terms. There are one or two dominant values that are more important than any others in the organization. People know that they cannot go far wrong as long as they are pursuing those values with sincerity and integrity.

- People do not argue much about the mission. People who do not share the organization's basic values and commitments are made to feel uncomfortable and usually leave.

- People do argue a lot about how best to achieve the mission. Positional authority does not shut off discussion or curb the expression of employees' ideas.

- The values embedded in the mission are larger than mere profit or growth. In pursuing the mission, organization members believe they are making a contribution to society, as well as gaining something for the company.

- The organization is more egalitarian than most. Employees are treated like willing contributors. Those at lower levels are empowered to make decisions that other organizations reserve for supervisors and middle managers.

- Communication channels are open, both laterally and vertically. It is easy to be heard if you have an idea or suggestion.

- Failure is viewed as something to learn from, rather than as a sign of personal inadequacy.

- People are given effective authority in accordance with their ability to contribute to the mission. Neither the red tape of a bureaucracy nor the privileges and status of a power elite count as much as ability and contribution in deciding who does what.

The Achievement-oriented organization has been called the *aligned* organization because it "lines people up" behind a common vision or purpose. It uses the mission to attract and release the personal energy of its members in the pursuit of common goals. The mission serves to focus the personal energy of individuals. Because members make their contributions freely in response to their commitment to a shared purpose, they willingly give more to the organization, and the whole prospers accordingly.

This inner commitment is in marked contrast to the Power- and Role-oriented organizations that rely on the application of rewards and punishment and on impersonal systems and structures to control and constrain their members.

Of course, structures and systems are still necessary in the Achievement-oriented organization, and the allocation and distribution of resources is still a problem. In such an organization, the systems and structures serve the mission and are changed when the mission requires it, rather than becoming laws unto themselves.

Power, too, has a place in such an organization. People in power generally establish the mission and then serve it. On a day-to-day basis, decisions are made by reference to the mission, not by reference to people in power. The actions of those in power are judged and criticized by the same standard as is applied to everyone else in the organization: do they advance the mission?

Enthusiasm for the hands-on, value-driven approach said to be typical of "excellent companies" has been so great that a negative side to the Achievement orientation may come as a surprise to some. The Achievement culture has the deficiencies and distortions brought on by its strengths. The high energy and involvement that are generated by the Achievement orientation are difficult to sustain, and organizational members are subject to burnout and disillusionment. Achievement organizations may rely on the common vision to organize the work, rather than subject themselves to the discipline of systems and procedures. When the task is complex and the vision takes on different forms for different parts of the organization, the organization may lose focus and unity of effort. When different groups each "do their own thing," coordination suffers and resources are wasted.

The following are some quotes from interviews with veterans of Achievement-oriented organizations in which hard work and long hours substitute for planning, the thrust for achievement has submerged concern for people's needs, and elitism and competition have eroded cooperation:

- We're too busy doing to plan objectively.

- There are bound to be organizational problems with tight resources and tight delivery schedules; things are bound to get tense. People who are attracted to our company like this climate; others would go loony here. Pressure is keen, and you have to compromise on quality sometimes.

- People are beginning to burn out; you can't keep putting the pressure on people. We must turn down our expectations of the magic we can perform and do more realistic scheduling.

- One of the craziest things about the company is the founders' ninety-hour weeks. My best people look like garbage by putting in only sixty-hour weeks.

- I'm worried about the health of some of the people; bad things are happening to the founders and old timers.

- Everyone needs positive feedback; even those who show outside self-confidence still like to hear the words. It's hard for many to say those words; it's easier for them to criticize than to stroke.

- We were team players inside and terribly competitive outside. People in other groups saw us as self-centered and uncooperative, and they were right. We really didn't care about anything but meeting our own objectives.

- Our arrogance and elitism isolated us from the rest of the organization. When we did make some mistakes, they were glad to see us fail.

- We became intolerant. We couldn't accept criticism either from outside the group or from our own members.

The Achievement-oriented organization is frequently underorganized; it relies on high motivation to overcome its deficiencies in structures, systems, and planning. Although it evokes enthusiasm and commitment, it may not have a heart. People's needs are subordinate to the organization's mission and its needs. After a time, people realize this and may begin to mistrust the organization—or they may remain committed but suffer high levels of emotional and physical stress. Under stress, organization members may withdraw into an idealistic fantasy world, losing touch with the realities of competition, customer needs, and the business environment (a fairly common phenomenon in R&D and high-tech organizations).

The Support Orientation

The Support culture may be defined as an organizational climate that is based on mutual trust between the individual and the organization. In such an organization, people believe that they are valued as human beings, not just as cogs in a machine or contributors to a task. A Support culture fosters warmth and even love, not just driving enthusiasm. People like to come to work in the morning, not only because they like their work but also because they care for the people with whom they work. Because they feel cared for, they are more human in their interactions with others: customers, suppliers, the public, and their fellow workers.

The Support-oriented organization may be characterized in the following ways:

- People help one another beyond the formal demands of their jobs. Help is extended not only within one's own work group, but to other groups as well.

- People communicate a lot, not only about work, but also about personal concerns. They can always find someone to listen to their ideas and problems.

- People like spending time together. They often see each other off the job, as well as on.

- In hiring people, the organization gives special weight to whether the person is caring and cooperative and will fit in.

- People are viewed as basically good. When things go wrong, they get a second chance.

- People know that the organization will go beyond the requirements of the policy or the employment contract to look after them when they need it. In return, they go out of their way to take care of the organization, caring for the facilities and equipment, giving special attention to quality, conserving resources, and/or protecting the company's reputation in the community.

- People celebrate together. They not only take pride in their work achievements, but they recognize such personal milestones as promotions, retirements, birthdays, and anniversaries.

- People value harmony and avoid confrontation, sometimes to the point of leaving important issues unresolved.

- People keep the faith; they don't let one another down. This does not mean merely keeping one's word; it also means doing one's share of the work, including coming in to work when one is not feeling quite up to par in order not to overload others.

In Western societies, the Support culture is the least typical of the four assessed by this instrument. It is not valued by the Power- or Role-oriented organizations, so it goes underground. It can be seen in relatively small groups, in which people know one another personally and interact face-to-face. It tends to develop in organizations in which people work together for long enough periods of time to build personal relationships, work out their differences, and arrive at a degree of trust.

When not balanced by a thrust for success, the pure Support culture seldom is found in business; it is not results-oriented enough to enable a business to be competitive. It makes its best contribution in dynamic tension with the Achievement orientation. The latter releases and focuses the personal energy that is evoked by a love of doing and by a sense of high purpose and worthy mission. The Support orientation taps into the emotional energy present in the ties of love and trust, which bind people to other people, groups, and organizations for which they care.

Two current issues in business show the benefits of a warm and caring organizational climate: quality and service. It is no accident that successful approaches to quality improvement are often based on small work teams. There is a close connection between loving one's work and wanting to do it well and having a sense of caring and trust with the people with whom one works. In teams dedicated to quality, people develop both a love of quality work and close ties with those with whom they work. When assembly operators who had left their jobs at one Fortune 500 company later reapplied for employment, they were asked why they decided to return. The most frequent reason was "I missed my quality circle!"

Like Achievement organizations, Support-oriented organizations assume that people want to contribute. Rather than evoking their contribution through a common purpose or ideal (a *doing* culture), the Support-oriented organization offers its members satisfactions that come from relationships: mutuality, belonging, and connection (a *being* culture). The assumption is that people will contribute out of a sense of commitment to a group or organization for which they feel a real sense of belonging and in which they believe they have a personal stake.

The emphasis on human needs of the Support culture balances and moderates the single-pointed task focus of the Achievement orientation. Where the one may use people up and burn them out, the other binds up their wounds, restores their energy and vitality, and heals their relationships. The Achievement culture unleashes and fuses the human will of organization members in the service of the organization's task. The Support culture evokes human love for the nurturing of the organization's members and the maintenance of the organization's essential fabric of relationships.

The Support culture can evoke extremely strong motivation in the service of the group. We see this motivation in the sacrifices that members of groups make for one another. The willingness of people to give their lives for those of their comrades is not only known in war, but also in close-knit teams doing dangerous work such as polar exploration, police work, and fire fighting. In more mundane work situations, the effects of team loyalty on productivity, quality, and absenteeism are well publicized in recent writing on high-performing organizations.

The weaknesses of the Support culture are the negative sides of its humanistic strengths. Organizations in which the Support culture is both strong and unbalanced tend toward conflict avoidance; in the interests of harmony, difficult issues are swept under the rug. Consensus may be overvalued, hampering the organization's ability to move decisively. Differences in skill and ability may be ignored in the interests of "equal treatment." Tough decisions about people's performance may be postponed out of "kindness," which negatively impacts the organization's effectiveness. In Power- and Role-oriented organizations, cohesive work teams also frequently support their members in anti-management behaviors, such as rate restriction and rule breaking.

UNDERSTANDING YOUR SCORES

In interpreting your scores, remember that the scores on the four scales are not completely independent, because you ranked the four alternatives on each question. The total possible points for the entire instrument is fixed at 300, so the higher your score on one scale, the lower your scores on the other scales.

Technically, then, you could have high scores on Power and low scores on Achievement and you would not be able to say for sure whether that means there is a lot of the Power orientation or just that the Achievement orientation is missing. In practice, it is not so difficult to tell, because there is usually a high degree of agreement among the members of an organization about what aspects of the culture they are responding to. Discussing your perceptions of the organization's orientation (and why you responded to the instrument the way you did) with other organizational members will reveal a great deal.

The Culture-Index scores are a useful way to summarize all four scales. By adding the Achievement and Support scores and subtracting those on the Power and Role scales, we obtain a measure that reflects the general level of empowerment, trust, and cooperation within the organization. It is easier to compare groups and organizations on one overall score than it is to consider four different scores. The Culture Index gives an indication of the extent to which people in the organization feel empowered and supported, versus controlled and constrained. It gives a rough measure of organizational enlivenment and good feeling. The Culture Index also is useful for comparing the organization's culture before and after some change, such as a merger, expansion, downsizing, introduction of total quality management, or some other process that is likely to shift values, attitudes, and behavior in the organization.

We would like to make a comment about our own cultural biases. It would be easy to read a bias toward the Achievement and Support cultures into our presentation, and to see it also in the phrasing of the items in the instrument. In fact, in constructing the instrument, we tried to write items that expressed the positive side of the Power and Role cultures and which would be seen by people as descriptive of their organizational experiences. That this task was difficult seems to us a reflection of the society in which we live, rather than of some inherent negativity in the concepts of Power and Role.

Power has the capacity to enliven life in organizations and to release the human spirit. There have been times in history when there has been a tradition of nobility and responsibility on the part of those who exercised power. In our own recent past, the concept of benevolent paternalism was much more prevalent than it is today. Conversations with those who have worked in Asia and Latin America suggest that responsible, caring power is much more common there than it is in the United States. In fact, we suspect that one of the secrets of Japanese success is the acceptance of inequality on the part of Japanese employees and the reciprocal acceptance of responsibility on the part of their leaders. The stability and mutual acceptance of one another's positions and prerogatives permits employees and leaders to work together without the power struggles that are such a frequent aspect of life in Western, Power-oriented organizations.

In the English-speaking world, people tend to have little love or respect for power or the people who wield it. Mirroring those negative attitudes, the power wielders often tend not to deserve love or loyalty. Those who do are seen as individual exceptions to the rule rather than as examples of a socially valued tradition. We do not know how to make organizations work without power; at the same time, we do not know how to trust power or make it trustworthy.

The situation of the Role-oriented organization is somewhat different. Traditionally, the systematic organization of work has been characterized by application of "scientific management" principles, top-down control, and faceless bureaucracy. Such Role-oriented organizations tend to squeeze the spirit out of working life, and the items in our Role scale have some of this flavor.

Working rationally and systematically does not inherently deaden the soul; it does so only when we elevate the system and the machine to the status of master and subordinate to it our creativity, vision, and human values. That working to improve systems and procedures can be enlivening is demonstrated by some of the work in sociotechnical systems design, total quality management, and employee involvement, where the emphasis is on making systems more responsive to the needs of the task (Achievement) and the people (Support) who work in the organization.

WHERE DO WE GO FROM HERE?

If we have a bias, it is toward the release of the human spirit in work. With Kahlil Gibran, we believe that "work is love made manifest" and that our organizations will be richer materially and spiritually to the extent that we can realize that dream. In reaching toward that ideal, organizations will do well to avoid dominance by any one of the four cultures and will choose instead a dynamic balance in which each culture is expressed in its highest form and the positive side of each balances the darker tendencies of the others. The ideal is not a compromise or average. It is a synthesis achieved by struggle and debate within the organization between different perceptions of what is good for the organization and for its stakeholders: employees, stockholders, customers, the community, and our planet.

We have designed Diagnosing Organizational Culture to be useful to anyone who wants to understand his or her organization better, whether or not he or she shares our vision. Below are some suggestions for how you can use the scores as the basis for dialogue with others in your organization about your own culture.

Conversations About Organizational Culture

One purpose of this instrument is to get people talking and sharing their insights about the cultures of their own organizations. It is designed to stimulate people to ask, "What are we like? How are we the same as or different from other organizations? Why are we the way we are? What do we like about being this way, and what would we like to change?" Your scores are signposts that can point to areas that are worth discussing.

You may want to determine how your scores compare with those from other organizations. You can do this by referring to the norms provided on pages 29 and 30. When a group's average score is higher than the seventy-fifth percentile or lower than the twenty-fifth percentile, the difference is worth noting and discussing.

Frequent Patterns of Culture in Organizations

Although every organization is different, some patterns come up again and again. These may apply to your organization.

One observation is that the scores on Power are negatively correlated with those on Achievement and Support. This means that if a group has a high score on Power, it tends to have low scores on both Achievement and Support. The Role scores tend to fluctuate fairly independently of the other scores.

The Power culture has a potential for fear and manipulation. People in Power-oriented cultures tend to be rather careful about what they say and to whom they say it. The Support and Achievement cultures require a fairly high degree of openness and trust to flourish. Therefore, we should expect an organization that is high on Power to be low on Achievement and Support.

If your organization has relatively high Power scores and rather low Support and Achievement scores, you may want to ask what is going on that makes it difficult for people to trust one another or the organization. When you try to have such a discussion in your organization, you may find it difficult. When people do not trust, one of the things they are afraid to do is to be open about how much trust they feel. This often causes people at the top of the organization to misread the thoughts and feelings of those lower in the hierarchy and to believe that people are happier about the state of affairs than is really the case. It usually is easier for people to discuss their true feelings with those on the same organizational level, so that is one way to begin. Do not be discouraged if it takes time to get communication going.

When people in an organization disagree about the culture they actually have, it often is because the culture looks and feels different from the perspective of different parts of the organization. It usually feels different at the top than it does at the bottom. Upper managers see more of the Achievement culture than do those lower down. The latter are more likely to see the organization as Power oriented.

Often, the kind of work people do and the way it is organized influence the culture of the group or department. Left to themselves, research and development groups tend to be Achievement oriented. Groups that keep track of and control money tend to be Role oriented. Marketing groups tend to be Achievement oriented, and sales organizations are more likely to have a Power culture. Production organizations tend toward a mix of Power and Role.

It is possible, however, to design organizations that have radically different cultures than those we have listed as norms. For example, the authors have seen sales organizations with an Achievement/Support culture that are as effective as or more effective than Power-oriented ones (and far more enjoyable for their members).

It is useful to discuss what kind of culture the members of your group would like to have and why your ideas of what would be best may differ. Such discussions are a good way to discover your own and others' values. If your values differ greatly, it helps to know that and to explore what is behind these differences.

If your cultural values, as expressed in the Preferred Culture scores, are similar, that may help you to find common ground in thinking about and planning where you want the organization to go. Often, organizational members find that their values are quite alike from the top to the bottom of the organization. Even though they may differ in their ideas about how they want to get there, they agree on where it is they want to go. From that base of agreement about the desired ends, it often is possible to resolve differences about the means.

NORMS FOR DIAGNOSING ORGANIZATIONAL CULTURE

Based on Sample in Research by
Roger Harrison and Herb Stokes

The table on page 29 allows you to find the percentile of each of your scores compared with the scores of 190 first-line and middle managers in our sample. The percentile of your score tells you what percent of the 190 middle managers had a lower score than you did. For example, suppose you had a score of 50 on Power. Locate 50 in the column labeled "Scores." The corresponding number in the column labeled "Power" is 70. This indicates that 70 percent of the people in our sample perceived their organization as having a lower Power orientation than you perceived for your organization. If you had a score of 50 on Role, however, the table shows that 94 percent of our sample perceived their organizations as having a lower Role orientation than you perceived for your organization. The average or mean score is indicated for each culture by an asterisk (*) in the corresponding row of the percentile columns. Percentiles for the scores on the **Preferred** cultures are on page 30.

SCORES	POWER	ROLE	ACHIEVEMENT	SUPPORT
16	0	0	0	2
17	0	0	0	3
18	3	0	0	5
19	5	0	0	6
20	5	1	0	10
21	6	2	0	12
22	7	2	1	18
23	8	2	1	22
24	10	3	2	25
25	11	4	2	33
26	12	4	2	35
27	13	4	2	37
28	15	5	5	45
29	18	6	6	50
30	20	10	15	*56
31	22	10	15	64
32	25	12	20	67
33	28	14	23	70
34	30	17	28	73
35	32	20	32	75
36	33	24	34	77
37	35	30	40	80
38	38	34	46	83
39	43	39	*48	85
40	46	*44	54	86
41	*47	50	56	86
42	51	55	60	87
43	56	60	63	88
44	59	67	66	88
45	60	78	71	88
46	62	84	74	88
47	66	88	77	90
48	67	90	80	90
49	68	91	87	90
50	70	94	90	90
51	72	97	93	90
52	75	97	95	91
53	78	98	96	92
54	82	99	98	92
55	84	100	100	93
56	85	100	100	95
57	88	100	100	97
58	90	100	100	97
59	95	100	100	98
60	98	100	100	99

PERCENTILES: Scores on *Preferred* Culture

SCORES	POWER	ROLE	ACHIEVEMENT	SUPPORT
16	2	0	0	0
17	7	0	1	0
18	12	0	2	0
19	22	0	3	0
20	30	1	4	1
21	37	3	5	1
22	44	3	6	2
23	56	3	6	3
24	58	3	6	4
25	61	3	7	6
26	66	3	8	7
27	*68	5	8	9
28	71	6	10	10
29	75	7	11	12
30	76	10	12	13
31	77	14	12	16
32	77	17	12	18
33	77	21	12	20
34	80	28	12	24
35	81	32	13	26
36	82	41	14	30
37	83	*47	14	37
38	84	52	14	*43
39	85	56	15	53
40	85	67	15	56
41	85	72	18	59
42	86	79	19	63
43	87	82	22	70
44	87	87	25	75
45	87	92	26	78
46	87	97	27	85
47	88	98	30	90
48	89	98	*34	90
49	89	98	36	92
50	89	99	40	92
51	90	99	44	94
52	90	99	49	96
53	90	99	56	97
54	91	99	61	98
55	92	100	70	98
56	92	100	77	99
57	93	100	85	99
58	95	100	90	99
59	98	100	95	99
60	99	100	99	99

Diagnosing Organizational Culture.